TEAM WORK
LOVE
WARM SMILES
SHARING
INCLUSION

LAUGHTER

KINDNESS

GIVING-
SECOND
CHANCES
HUGGS
PLAYING

FRIENDSHIP

TAKING TURNS
FUN
COMPASSION
UNDER-
STANDING

PLAYDATES

STORYTELLING

HELPING
HONESTY
CONNECTION
SAYING-
SORRY
CARING

This book belongs to:

....

....

This book belongs to:

....

....

People also call me:

....

My age:

My Birthday

Home address:

telephone number:

email :

Please place your picture here

My favorite food:

color my favorite color

My school (class) name: ....

My teacher's name: ....

My favorite toy:

☐ ☐ ☐ ☐

☐ Other: ....

My favorite animal: ....

My favorite thing to do: ....

....

My favorite book: ....

My favorite TV show (movie): ....

....

3 words that best describe me: ....

....

My favorite song: ....

What I do not like: ....

....

What I can do:

☐   ☐ 123   ☐ Name

☐ abc   ☐   ☐

☐ Other: ....

I drew this:

What I want to be when I grow up: ....
....
What I wish: ....
....
My signature: ....

Please place your picture here

My name is: ....

My age: **1** 2 3 4 5 6 7 8 9

My birthday: ....

Phone number: ....

Email: ....

color my favorite color

My address: ....

....

My school (class) name: ....

My teacher's name: ....

3 words that best describe me: ....

My favorite animal: ....

My favorite toy: ....

My favorite thing to do: ....

My favorite book: ....

My favorite food: ....

My favorite TV show (movie): ....

I drew this for you:

What I do not like: ....

What I can do: ....

What I want to be when I grow up: ....

What I like about you: ....

I wish you: ....

My signature: ....

My name is:..
....

My age: **1 2 3 4 5 6 7 8 9**

My birthday: ....

Phone number: ....

Email: ....

My address: ....

....

My school (class) name: ....

My teacher's name: ....

My favorite toy: ....

3 words that best describe me: ....

My favorite thing to play: ....

My favorite book: ....

My favorite food: ....

My favorite animal: ....

My favorite TV show (movie): ....

Please place your picture here

color my favorite color

What I do not like: ....

What I can do: ....

What I want to be when I grow up: ....

What I like about you: ....

I drew this for you:

I wish you: ....

My signature: ....

Please place
your picture here

My name is: ....

....

My age: 1 2 3 4 5 6 7 8 9

My birthday: ....

Phone number: ....

Email: ....

My address: ....

....

My school (class) name: ....

My teacher's name: ....

3 words that best describe me: ....

My favorite toy: ....

My favorite thing to play: ....

My favorite book: ....

My favorite food: ....

My favorite animal: ....

My favorite TV show (movie): ....

I drew this for you:

What I do not like: ....

What I can do: ....

What I want to be when I grow up: ....

What I like about you: ....

I wish you: ....

My signature: ....

color my favorite color

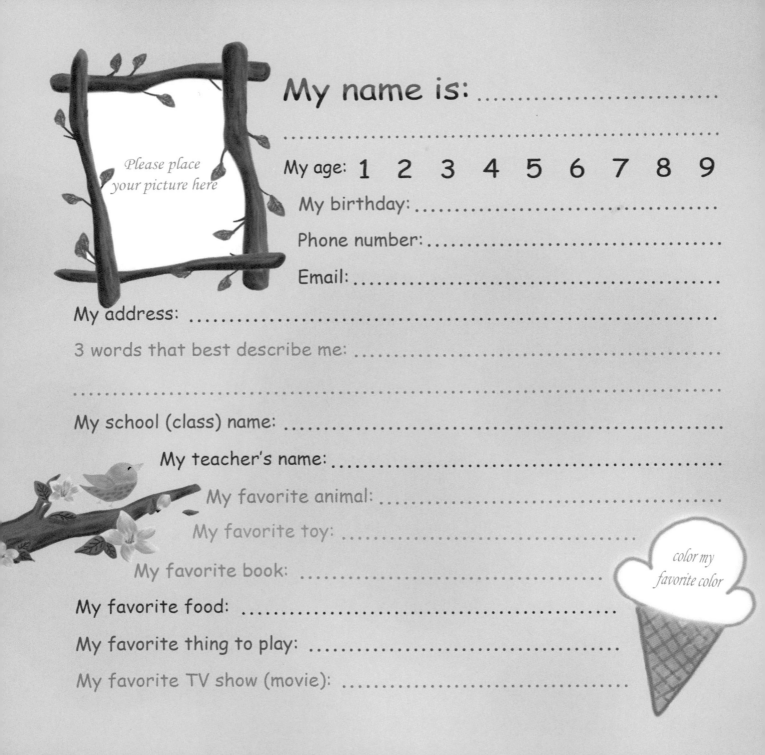

My name is: ....

....

My age: **1** **2** **3** **4** **5** **6** **7** **8** **9**

My birthday: ....

Phone number: ....

Email: ....

My address: ....

3 words that best describe me: ....

....

My school (class) name: ....

My teacher's name: ....

My favorite animal: ....

My favorite toy: ....

My favorite book: ....

My favorite food: ....

My favorite thing to play: ....

My favorite TV show (movie): ....

Please place your picture here

color my favorite color

I drew this for you:

What I do not like: ....

What I can do: ....

What I want to be when I grow up: ....

What I like about you: ....

I wish you: ....

My signature: ....

Please place
your picture here

My name is: ....

....

My age: 1 2 3 4 5 6 7 8 9

My birthday: ....

Phone number: ....

Email: ....

My address: ....

My school (class) name: ....

My teacher's name: ....

3 words that best describe me: ....

....

My favorite thing to play: ....

My favorite toy: ....

My favorite book: ....

My favorite food: ....

My favorite animal: ....

My favorite TV show (movie): ....

I drew this for you:

What I do not like: ....

What I can do: ....

What I want to be when I grow up: ....

What I like about you: ....

I wish you: ....

My signature: ....

color my favorite color

Please place your picture here

My name is: ....
....

My age: **1 2 3 4 5 6 7 8 9**

My birthday: ....

Phone number: ....

Email: ....

color my favorite color

My address: ....
....

My school (class) name: ....

My teacher's name: ....

My favorite toy: ....

3 words that best describe me: ......

My favorite thing to do: ....

My favorite book: ....

My favorite food: ....

My favorite animal: ....

My favorite TV show (movie): ....

What I do not like: ....

What I can do: ....

What I want to be when I grow up: ....

What I like about you: ....

I drew this for you:

I wish you: ....

My signature: ....

My name is: ....
....

Please place your picture here

My age: **1 2 3 4 5 6 7 8 9**

My birthday: ....

Phone number: ....

Email: ....

My address: ....
....

My school (class) name: ....

My teacher's name: ....

3 words that best describe me: ....

My favorite toy: ....

My favorite thing to play: ....

My favorite book: ....

My favorite food: ....

My favorite animal: ....

My favorite TV show (movie): ....

I drew this for you:

What I do not like: ....

What I can do: ....

What I want to be when I grow up: ....

What I like about you: ....

I wish you: ....

My signature: ....

color my favorite color

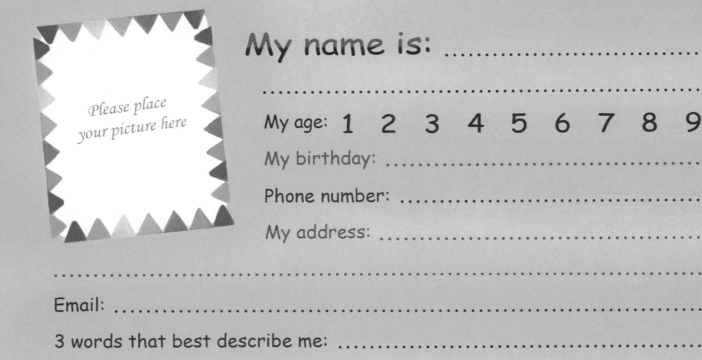

Please place your picture here

My name is: ....

....

My age: 1 2 3 4 5 6 7 8 9

My birthday: ....

Phone number: ....

My address: ....

....

Email: ....

3 words that best describe me: ....

My school (class) name: ....

My teacher's name: ....

My favorite toy: ....

My favorite book: ....

My favorite animal: ....

My favorite food: ....

My favorite thing to play: ....

My favorite TV show (movie): ....

color my favorite color

What I do not like: ....

What I can do: ....

What I want to be when I grow up: ....

What I like about you: ....

I wish you: ....

My signature: ....

Please place your picture here

My name is: ....
....

My age: **1 2 3 4 5 6 7 8 9**

My birthday: ....

Phone number: ....

Email: ....

My address: ....

My school (class) name: ....

My teacher's name: ....

3 words that best describe me: ....
....

My favorite toy: ....

My favorite book: ....

My favorite thing to play: ....

My favorite food: ....

My favorite animal: ....

My favorite TV show (movie): ....

color my favorite color

I drew this for you:

What I do not like: ....

What I can do: ....

What I want to be when I grow up: ....

What I like about you: ....

I wish you: ....

My signature: ....

Please place your picture here

My name is: ....
....

My age: **1   2   3   4   5   6   7   8   9**

My birthday: ....

My phone number: ....

Email: ....

My address: ....
....

color my favorite color

My school (class) name: ....

My teacher's name: ....

My favorite toy: ....

My favorite thing to play: ....

3 words that best describe me: ....

My favorite book: ....

My favorite food: ....

My favorite animal: ....

My favorite TV show (movie): ....

What I like about you: ....

What I can do: ....

What I want to be when I grow up: ....

What I do not like: ....

I drew this for you:

I wish you: ....

My signature: ....

My name is: ....
....

My age: **1 2 3 4 5 6 7 8 9**

My birthday: ....

Phone number: ....

Email: ....

color my favorite color

My address: ....

My school (class) name: ....

My teacher's name: ....

3 words that best describe me: ....
....

My favorite toy: ....

My favorite thing to play: ....

My favorite book: ....

My favorite food: ....

My favorite animal: ....

My favorite TV show (movie): ....

What I do not like: ....

What I can do: ....

What I want to be when I grow up: ....

What I like about you: ....

I wish you: ....

My signature: ....

Please place your picture here

My name is: ....
....

My age: **1 2 3 4 5 6 7 8 9**

My birthday: ....

My phone number: ....

Email: ....

My address: ....

My school (class) name: ....

My teacher's name: ....

3 words that best describe me: ....
....

My favorite toy: ....

My favorite book: ....

My favorite thing to play: ....

My favorite food: ....

My favorite animal: ....

My favorite TV show (movie): ....

color my favorite color

I drew this for you:

What I do not like: ....

What I can do: ....

What I want to be when I grow up: ....

What I like about you: ....

I wish you: ....

My signature: ....

Please place your picture here

My name is: ....
....

My age: **1 2 3 4 5 6 7 8 9**

My birthday: ....

Phone number: ....

Email: ....

color my favorite color

My address: ....
....

My school (class) name: ....

My teacher's name: ....

3 words that best describe me: ....

My favorite animal: ....

My favorite toy: ....

My favorite thing to do: ....

My favorite book: ....

My favorite food: ....

My favorite TV show (movie): ....

I drew this for you!

What I do not like: ....

What I can do: ....

What I want to be when I grow up: ....

What I like about you: ....

I wish you: ....

My signature: ....

My name is: ....
....

My age: 1 2 3 4 5 6 7 8 9

My birthday: ....

Phone number: ....

Email: ....

My address: ....
....

My school (class) name: ....

My teacher's name: ....

My favorite toy: ....

3 words that best describe me: ....

My favorite thing to play: ....

My favorite book: ....

My favorite food: ....

My favorite animal: ....

My favorite TV show (movie): ....

Please place your picture here

color my favorite color

What I do not like: ....

What I can do: ....

What I want to be when I grow up: ....

What I like about you: ....

I drew this for you:

I wish you: ....

My signature: ....

My name is: ....
....

My age: **1 2 3 4 5 6 7 8 9**

My birthday: ....

Phone number: ....

Email: ....

My address: ....

My school (class) name: ....

My teacher's name: ....

3 words that best describe me: ....

My favorite toy: ....

My favorite thing to play: ....

My favorite book: ....

My favorite food: ....

My favorite animal: ....

My favorite TV show (movie): ....

Please place your picture here

I drew this for you:

What I do not like: ....

What I can do: ....

What I want to be when I grow up: ....

What I like about you: ....

I wish you: ....

My signature: ....

color my favorite color

Please place your picture here

My name is: ....

....

My age: **1 2 3 4 5 6 7 8 9**

My birthday: ....

Phone number: ....

Email: ....

My address: ....

3 words that best describe me: ....

....

My school (class) name: ....

My teacher's name: ....

My favorite animal: ....

My favorite toy: ....

My favorite book: ....

My favorite food: ....

My favorite thing to play: ....

My favorite TV show (movie): ....

color my favorite color

I drew this for you:

What I do not like: ....

What I can do: ....

What I want to be when I grow up: ....

What I like about you: ....

I wish you: ....

My signature: ....

My name is: ....

....

My age: 1 2 3 4 5 6 7 8 9

My birthday: ....

Phone number: ....

Email: ....

My address: ....

My school (class) name: ....

My teacher's name: ....

3 words that best describe me: ....

....

My favorite thing to play: ....

My favorite toy: ....

My favorite book: ....

My favorite food: ....

My favorite animal: ....

My favorite TV show (movie): ....

I drew this for you:

What I do not like: ....

What I can do: ....

What I want to be when I grow up: ....

What I like about you: ....

I wish you: ....

My signature: ....

color my favorite color

Please place your picture here

My name is: ....
....

My age: 1 2 3 4 5 6 7 8 9

My birthday: ....

Phone number: ....

Email: ....

My address: ....
....

My school (class) name: ....

My teacher's name: ....

My favorite toy: ....

3 words that best describe me: ....

My favorite thing to do: ....

My favorite book: ....

My favorite food: ....

My favorite animal: ....

My favorite TV show (movie): ....

color my favorite color

What I do not like: ....

What I can do: ....

What I want to be when I grow up: ....

What I like about you: ....

I drew this for you:

I wish you: ....

My signature: ....

My name is: ....

....

My age: **1 2 3 4 5 6 7 8 9**

My birthday: ....

Phone number: ....

Email: ....

My address: ....

Please place your picture here

....

My school (class) name: ....

My teacher's name: ....

3 words that best describe me: ....

My favorite toy: ....

My favorite thing to play: ....

My favorite book: ....

My favorite food: ....

My favorite animal: ....

My favorite TV show (movie): ....

I drew this for you:

What I do not like: ....

What I can do: ....

What I want to be when I grow up: ....

What I like about you: ....

I wish you: ....

My signature: ....

color my favorite color

Please place your picture here

My name is: ....
....

My age: **1   2   3   4   5   6   7   8   9**

My birthday: ....

Phone number: ....

My address: ....
....

Email: ....

3 words that best describe me: ....

My school (class) name: ....

My teacher's name: ....

My favorite toy: ....

My favorite book: ....

color my favorite color

My favorite animal: ....

My favorite food: ....

My favorite thing to play: ....

My favorite TV show (movie): ....

What I do not like: ....

What I can do: ....

What I want to be when I grow up: ....

What I like about you: ....

I wish you: ....

My signature: ....

Please place your picture here

My name is: ....
....

My age: **1 2 3 4 5 6 7 8 9**

My birthday: ....

Phone number: ....

Email: ....

My address: ....

My school (class) name: ....

My teacher's name: ....

3 words that best describe me: ....
....

My favorite toy: ....

My favorite book: ....

My favorite thing to play: ....

My favorite food: ....

My favorite animal: ....

My favorite TV show (movie): ....

color my favorite color

I drew this for you:

What I do not like: ....

What I can do: ....

What I want to be when I grow up: ....

What I like about you: ....

I wish you: ....

My signature: ....

Please place your picture here

My name is: ....

....

My age: 1 2 3 4 5 6 7 8 9

My birthday: ....

Phone number: ....

Email: ....

My address: ....

....

My school (class) name: ....

My teacher's name: ....

My favorite toy: ....

My favorite thing to play: ....

3 words that best describe me: ....

My favorite book: ....

My favorite food: ....

My favorite animal: ....

My favorite TV show (movie): ....

color my favorite color

What I like about you: ....

What I can do: ....

What I want to be when I grow up: ....

What I do not like: ....

I drew this for you:

I wish you: ....

My signature: ....

My name is: ....

....

My age: **1** **2** **3** **4** **5** **6** **7** **8** **9**

My birthday: ....

Phone number: ....

Email: ....

color my favorite color

My address: ....

My school (class) name: ....

My teacher's name: ....

3 words that best describe me: ....

....

My favorite toy: ....

My favorite thing to play: ....

 My favorite book: ....

My favorite food: ....

My favorite animal: ....

My favorite TV show (movie): ....

What I do not like: ....

What I can do: ....

What I want to be when I grow up: ....

What I like about you: ....

I wish you: ....

My signature: ....

Please place your picture here

My name is: ....

....

My age: **1 2 3 4 5 6 7 8 9**

My birthday: ....

Phone number: ....

Email: ....

My address: ....

My school (class) name: ....

My teacher's name: ....

3 words that best describe me: ....

....

My favorite toy: ....

My favorite book: ....

My favorite thing to play: ....

My favorite food: ....

My favorite animal: ....

My favorite TV show (movie): ....

color my favorite color

I drew this for you:

What I do not like: ....

What I can do: ....

What I want to be when I grow up: ....

What I like about you: ....

I wish you: ....

My signature: ....

My name is: ....

....

My age: **1** 2 3 4 5 6 7 8 9

My birthday: ....

Phone number: ....

Email: ....

color my favorite color

My address: ....

....

My school (class) name: ....

My teacher's name: ....

3 words that best describe me: ....

My favorite animal: ....

My favorite toy: ....

My favorite thing to do: ....

My favorite book: ....

My favorite food: ....

My favorite TV show (movie): ....

I drew this for you:

What I do not like: ....

What I can do: ....

What I want to be when I grow up: ....

What I like about you: ....

I wish you: ....

My signature: ....

My name is: ....
....

My age: 1 2 3 4 5 6 7 8 9

My birthday: ....

Phone number: ....

Email: ....

My address: ....
....

My school (class) name: ....

My teacher's name: ....

My favorite toy: ....

3 words that best describe me: ....

My favorite thing to play: ....

My favorite book: ....

My favorite food: ....

My favorite animal: ....

My favorite TV show (movie): ....

Please place your picture here

color my favorite color

What I do not like: ....

What I can do: ....

What I want to be when I grow up: ....

What I like about you: ....

I drew this for you:

I wish you: ....

My signature: ....

My name is: ....

....

My age: 1 2 3 4 5 6 7 8 9

My birthday: ....

Phone number: ....

Email: ....

My address: ....

....

Please place
your picture here

My school (class) name: ....

My teacher's name: ....

3 words that best describe me: ....

My favorite toy: ....

My favorite thing to play: ....

My favorite book: ....

My favorite food: ....

My favorite animal: ....

My favorite TV show (movie): ....

I drew this for you:

What I do not like: ....

What I can do: ....

What I want to be when I grow up: ....

What I like about you: ....

I wish you: ....

My signature: ....

color my favorite color

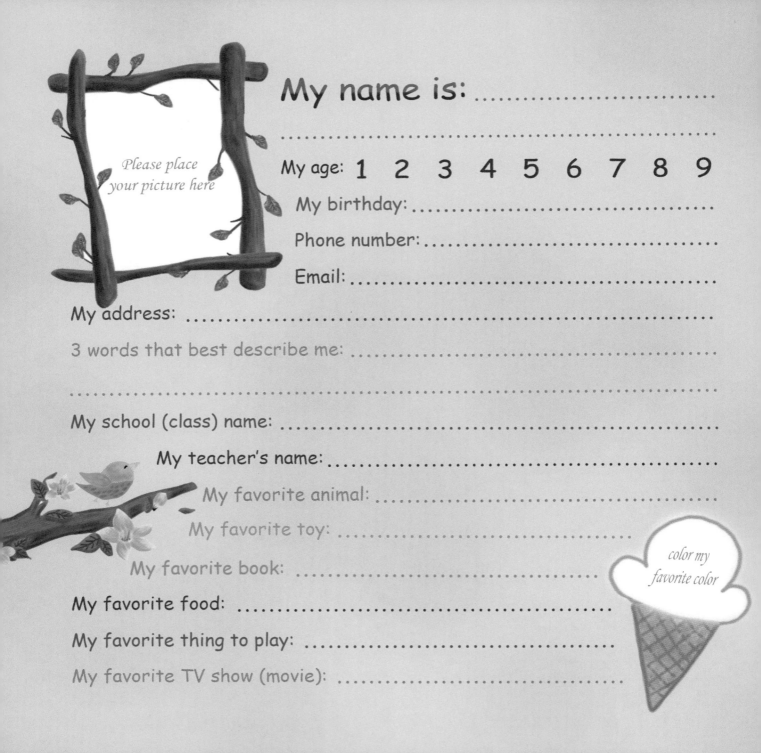

Please place your picture here

My name is: ....

....

My age: **1   2   3   4   5   6   7   8   9**

My birthday: ....

Phone number: ....

Email: ....

My address: ....

3 words that best describe me: ....

....

My school (class) name: ....

My teacher's name: ....

My favorite animal: ....

My favorite toy: ....

My favorite book: ....

My favorite food: ....

My favorite thing to play: ....

My favorite TV show (movie): ....

color my favorite color

I drew this for you:

What I do not like: ....

What I can do: ....

What I want to be when I grow up: ....

What I like about you: ....

I wish you: ....

My signature: ....

My name is: ....

....

My age: **1 2 3 4 5 6 7 8 9**

My birthday: ....

Phone number: ....

Email: ....

My address: ....

My school (class) name: ....

My teacher's name: ....

3 words that best describe me: ....

....

My favorite thing to play: ....

My favorite toy: ....

My favorite book: ....

My favorite food: ....

My favorite animal: ....

My favorite TV show (movie): ....

I drew this for you:

What I do not like: ....

What I can do: ....

What I want to be when I grow up: ....

What I like about you: ....

I wish you: ....

My signature: ....

color my favorite color

Please place your picture here

My name is: ....
....

My age: **1 2 3 4 5 6 7 8 9**

My birthday: ....

Phone number: ....

Email: ....

My address: ....

....

My school (class) name: ....

My teacher's name: ....

My favorite toy: ....

3 words that best describe me: ....

My favorite thing to do: ....

My favorite book: ....

My favorite food: ....

My favorite animal: ....

My favorite TV show (movie): ....

color my favorite color

What I do not like: ....

What I can do: ....

What I want to be when I grow up: ....

What I like about you: ....

I drew this for you:

I wish you: ....

My signature: ....

My name is: ....

....

My age: **1 2 3 4 5 6 7 8 9**

My birthday: ....

Phone number: ....

Email: ....

My address: ....

....

Please place your picture here

My school (class) name: ....

My teacher's name: ....

3 words that best describe me: ....

My favorite toy: ....

My favorite thing to play: ....

My favorite book: ....

My favorite food: ....

My favorite animal: ....

My favorite TV show (movie): ....

I drew this for you:

What I do not like: ....

What I can do: ....

What I want to be when I grow up: ....

What I like about you: ....

I wish you: ....

My signature: ....

color my favorite color

Please place your picture here

My name is: ....
....

My age: **1   2   3   4   5   6   7   8   9**

My birthday: ....

Phone number: ....

My address: ....

....

Email: ....

3 words that best describe me: ....

My school (class) name: ....

My teacher's name: ....

My favorite toy: ....

My favorite book: ....

My favorite animal: ....

My favorite food: ....

My favorite thing to play: ....

My favorite TV show (movie): ....

color my favorite color

What I do not like: ....

What I can do: ....

What I want to be when I grow up: ....

What I like about you: ....

I wish you: ....

My signature: ....

Please place your picture here

My name is: ....
....

My age: **1 2 3 4 5 6 7 8 9**

My birthday: ....

Phone number: ....

Email: ....

My address: ....

My school (class) name: ....

My teacher's name: ....

3 words that best describe me: ....
....

My favorite toy: ....

My favorite book: ....

My favorite thing to play: ....

My favorite food: ....

My favorite animal: ....

My favorite TV show (movie): ....

color my favorite color

I drew this for you:

What I do not like: ....

What I can do: ....

What I want to be when I grow up: ....

What I like about you: ....

I wish you: ....

My signature: ....

Made in the USA
Middletown, DE
14 May 2022

65783747R00042